CALIFORNIA

Copyright © 1988 Raintree Publishers Limited Partnership

A Turner Educational Services, Inc. book. Based on the Portrait
of America television series created by R.E. (Ted) Turner.

Library of Congress Number: 87-16395

4567890   99989796959493929190

Library of Congress Cataloging in Publication Data

Thompson, Kathleen.
  California.

  (Portrait of America)
  "A Turner book."
  Summary: Discusses the history, economy, culture,
and future of California. Also includes a state
chronology, pertinent statistics, and maps.
    1. California—Juvenile literature. [1. California]
I. Title. II. Series: Thompson, Kathleen.
Portrait of America.
F861.3.T48 1987   979.4   87-16395
ISBN 0-86514-462-1 (lib. bdg.)
ISBN 0-86514-537-7 (softcover)

Cover Photo: Redwood Empire Assn.

★ ★ ★ ★
Portrait of AMERICA

CALIFORNIA

Kathleen Thompson

A TURNER BOOK
RAINTREE PUBLISHERS

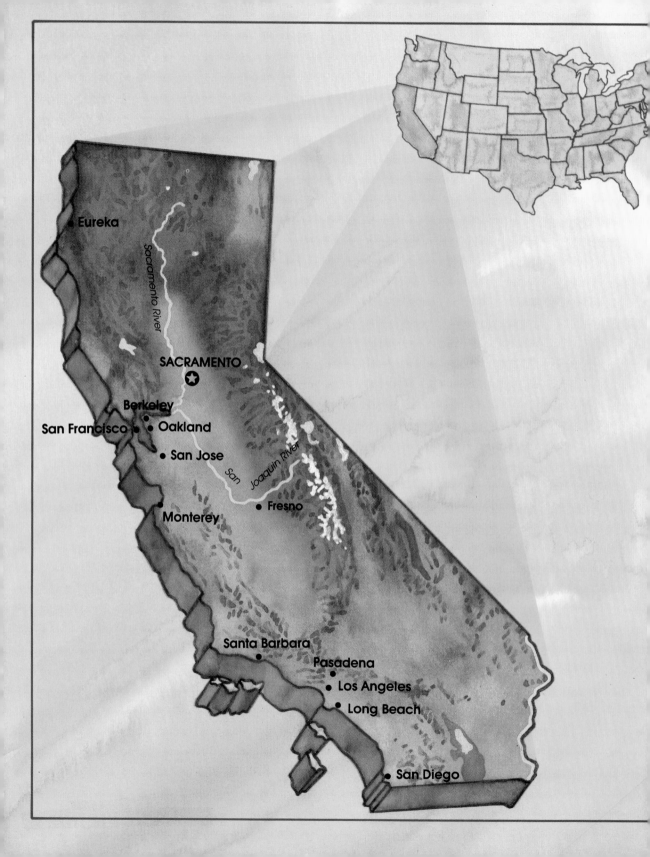

CONTENTS

Introduction

California, the Golden State.

"I think in California you can really be yourself all the time."

California: farms, oil wells, Hollywood, sunshine, orchards, dreams.

"I think we prefer illusion over reality here because we've discovered we know too much about reality and we have to find ways of making do with it."

California is a glittering place. From the gold dug out of its earth to the glaring lights of the movie studios to the ever faithful sun, California shines with promise. It has been called the place where old dreams go to die. It is also the place where millions of dreams are born.

San Francisco's Golden Gate Bridge.

Under Two Flags

In the years before white settlers came to California, the people who lived in this vast and beautiful region were Indians. They lived where the land was rich and fertile. One tribe was usually separated from another not only by culture and language but by deserts and mountains. Later, missionaries would come, people who believed that the Indians should give up the religion and the way of life that had been theirs for thousands of years. Backed by the force of Spanish weapons, those missionaries would come close to destroying forever these native American cultures. But for now, in the early 1500s, the Indians lived in peace.

In 1540, a Spanish explorer named Hernando de Alarcón discovered the lower Colorado River. The group he was with

Built in 1769, Mission San Diego de Alcala is the oldest of California's mission churches.

saw California but did not explore it. The first European to explore any part of the region was Juan Rodriguez Cabrillo. He and Bartolomé Ferrelo—who went on after Cabrillo died—probably explored the entire coastline.

These first explorers were looking for two things: gold and a way to go from the Atlantic to the Pacific by boat. They found neither and went back home.

In 1579, Sir Francis Drake, a very famous English explorer, repaired his ships in Trinidad or Bodega Bay on his way around the world. About twenty years later, Sebastián Vizcaíno explored the coast carefully and reported back to Spain that California should be colonized, but nothing happened for almost another hundred years. In fact, people thought for a long time that California was really a group of islands.

Then, in 1697, Jesuit missionaries came into Lower California, the Mexican peninsula south of what is now the state of California. They set up missions where they attempted to convert the people of California to a belief in Christianity. The Jesuits remained in Lower California until 1767. In that year, Charles III of Spain took their property from them and gave it to Franciscan monks, who were there for only three years before the Dominicans took over the missions. At that point, the Franciscans moved north into Upper California, what is now the state of California.

In the meantime, Russia had shown signs of interest in Upper

At right is a map drawn by Sebastián Vizcaíno in 1603. The map shows the coastline around what is now San Francisco, but omits San Francisco Bay, which had not yet been discovered. Below is La Jolla Cove in San Diego.

San Diego Convention & Visitors Bureau

California. Spain began to get worried. The Spanish government set up outposts at San Diego and Monterey. California was now considered a part of New Spain—at least, by the Spaniards.

From 1769 to 1823, the Franciscans built missions in Upper California. These missions were not just churches. They raised cattle, for example, and traded the hides and tallow to foreign countries. The Indians whose souls were supposedly being saved were used very much like slaves at the missions. Many of them died of illness and overwork.

In 1810 there was a revolution in Mexico against Spain. Upper and Lower California, however, remained loyal to Spain. But when Mexico won its independence in 1822, California went with it.

All of California—Upper and Lower—was now a part of the newly free country. But the people were not happy with the situation. The Mexican government had good plans, but no money. There was little they could do for the provinces, especially after Californians started rebelling. Between 1831 and 1845, four Mexican governors were driven out of office in California. To make matters worse, there was jealousy between Upper and Lower California.

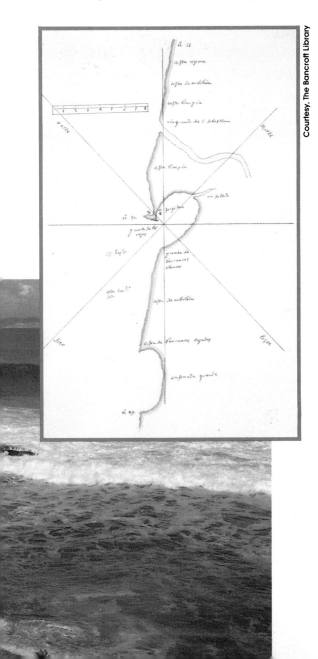

Courtesy, The Bancroft Library

Mexico had to fight other influences in California as well. Californians traded freely with other countries. They'd done it when they were part of New Spain in spite of Spanish laws. They did it now in spite of Mexican laws.

The Russians traded with Californians at the post called Fort Ross that they set up in 1812. They remained there until 1841. In 1826, traders and trappers from the United States traveled overland to California. The first was a man named Jedediah Strong Smith, but many others followed, including Kit Carson. In 1830, the Hudson's Bay Company set up operations in the northern part of Upper California. After about 1840, immigrants from the U.S. to California were numerous. Many of them became Mexican citizens and were given land. Some married into old California families.

The most important of these new immigrants was a man named John A. Sutter. Sutter had a grant of about 50,000 acres, and he built himself a fort there. He was Swiss himself, but many U.S. citizens gathered at his fort.

California accepted U.S. citizens graciously, but more and more, these newcomers wanted

Photos L.A. Co. Natural History Museum

to break away from Mexico. Some wanted California to become an independent republic. Some wanted the province to become a U.S. state. In 1835, President Andrew Jackson offered to buy the northern part of California. His offer was turned down. In 1845, the U.S. consul at Monterey, Thomas O. Larkin, was instructed to work towards the day when California would withdraw from Mexico. At the same time, U.S. naval officers were told to occupy California ports, just in case there was war with Mexico.

Then Captain J. C. Frémont came onto the scene. Captain Frémont's job was surveying for the U.S. government. However, his actions looked suspiciously military to the California authorities. In the end, he broke the peace, seized a group of Mexican cavalry mounts, and encouraged a group of U.S. settlers to take over the province's northern headquarters at Sonoma.

Above is John A. Sutter. Below is a view of Sutter's Fort as it appeared in 1847. The fort was located near what is now Sacramento.

Above, a group of prospectors uses a sluice box filled with water to sift shovelfuls of earth for gold nuggets.

This rebellious group of pioneers and frontiersmen promptly lowered the Mexican flag and raised another over the fort. And it was not the flag of the United States that they hoisted into the air. It was a homemade banner decorated with a bear, a star, and the words *California Republic*. They were ready to declare California's independence.

What this little group didn't know was that Mexico and the United States had gone to war one month before. The two countries were fighting primarily about Texas, not California, but the result of the war would be that both would become part of the United States of America.

Just before Mexico and the United States signed the Treaty of Guadalupe Hidalgo, making California a part of the U.S., something changed the area's future. A carpenter named James W. Marshall was building a mill on John A. Sutter's land, on the American River. On the site of the mill, he discovered gold—nuggets of gold.

Suddenly, California was flooded with people looking for gold. They came by the thousands, hungry for sudden wealth. In July of 1850 there were 500 ships stranded in San Francisco Bay because their sailors had gone to look for gold. Soldiers deserted

At right is James W. Marshall. The photograph in the background shows Marshall as a young man, standing in front of Sutter's mill.

from the army. Storekeepers closed their stores. About 80,000 people came to California in 1849 alone. It would not be the last time that people flocked from all over the country to California looking for wealth.

A strong government was needed more than ever before— and California didn't have it. Gold had made California important. Slavery and the anti-slavery forces had made every act of Congress with regard to new ter-

ritory a fight to the death. So no real government was created for California until 1850, when the area was admitted to the union as a state. In the meantime, the west was never wilder.

The miners made money hand over fist and they spent it as fast as they made it. There was no home life in the state because there were almost no women. Almost 92 percent of the population was male. In the mining area, the percentage was 98.

During this time, gold turned San Francisco into a glittering city. Gold built theaters and stores. The men who didn't find gold built farms.

People continued to pour into California for years. In 1860, the state's population was almost 400,000.

When the Civil War came, California remained in the Union. After the war, there was another rush of people into the state. Instead of gold, they were looking for cheap land and high wages.

Then trouble came. The gold rush, the war, and the building of the Central Pacific Railroad had created a lot of jobs in California. In 1870, the mining was slowing down, the war was over, and the railroad was built. Jobs became scarce. Then the Central Pacific fired 15,000 Chinese workers who were no longer needed to lay the tracks.

When those Chinese workers flooded San Francisco looking for

More than 15,000 Chinese laborers helped build the Central Pacific Railroad. Below is a photograph taken during the construction of a trestle over Secrettown Ravine, about 64 miles east of Sacramento.

Some of the devastation caused by the San Francisco earthquake of 1906. The Valencia Hotel (above) sank six feet into the earth when an underground streambed collapsed beneath it.

work, riots broke out. White workers blamed their unemployment on the Chinese. In 1870, a law was passed forbidding Chinese immigrants to enter this country. The Chinese people who were already in California were discriminated against and abused.

California continued to grow. In the 1880s there was a real estate boom and a third rush of people came into the state.

Disaster hit in 1906. San Francisco was almost completely destroyed by a huge earthquake and the fires that followed. But the city began building again immediately.

Also in 1906, there began to be hostility to Japanese immigrants. In 1913, a law was passed preventing Japanese people from owning land in California. After that, the United States and Japan made an agreement that no more Japanese people would immigrate to America. This policy lasted for many years.

By this time, gold mining was no longer the basis of California's economy. Because of irrigation, farming was growing rapidly. In 1890, a million acres of land were being irrigated. By 1920, that figure had grown to almost four million. Manufacturing began to grow after oil fields were opened. And, of course, there were the movies. By 1910, Hollywood had become the movie capital of the world.

In the 1930s came the Great Depression. California was not hit as hard as most of the country at first. But then came the fourth flood of people into the state. These people came from the Dust Bowl states. During the great drought, they had lost their farms and shops. The banks had taken away their homes. They had nothing but what they could carry with them. They came to California looking for work and they would work for anything. As a result, many Californians lost their jobs. Soon California passed a variety of laws to deal with the poor.

When the United States entered World War II, California became a center of aircraft manufacturing. The economy of the state prospered. Discrimination against Asians came up again, though, after the Japanese attack on Pearl Harbor in 1941. The United States government herded thousands

On the set of a silent era Hollywood western. This photo was taken around 1910. Galleries above the stage allow spectators to observe the actors and crew during filming.

During World War II, California factories produced aircraft for the war effort. Above, a worker at Lockheed during final assembly of a P-38 fighter.

of American citizens of Japanese ancestry into internment camps where they remained until the end of the war.

After World War II many people who had been stationed there in the armed forces decided to stay. The economy boomed. At the same time, the state government had to rise to the challenge of building more schools and roads and other services for the people. Also, with more factories came more dirt—in the water and in the air. The word *smog* was invented to describe California air.

In the 1960s, in the United States, centuries of terrible treatment for the black people in our country were coming to an end. But when things change, there are often problems. California, like most of the states, experienced violence during the Civil Rights movement. In 1965, there were riots in the Watts section of Los Angeles.

Two politicians who began their careers in California later became president. Richard M. Nixon was elected in 1968 and 1972. He resigned the office in 1974 because of the Watergate scandal. Ronald Reagan was elected in 1980 and again in 1984.

A major earthquake again hit California in 1971. It was not as serious as the San Francisco earthquake of 1906, but sixty-four people in and around Los Angeles were killed.

Today, California is still growing. It is a worldwide center for entertainment and education. It is one of the most important agricultural, manufacturing, and mining areas in the country. And, for thousands of people all over the world, it is the place where dreams come true.

Something Special

"On rainy days, I would just lie in my bed and I would think about probably being the first woman to go to the moon. . . . I wanted to be something special, something where my parents could look back and say, 'Hey, that's our daughter and we're proud of her.'"

Cheryl Miller hasn't gone to the moon, but there is no denying that she is special. She is a young woman any parents could be proud of. She's a tall, strong, beautiful woman who plays basketball like Wilt Chamberlain.

Cheryl Miller is one of the best woman basketball players who ever lived. And she has an Olympic Gold Medal to prove it. She worked hard and did what she always dreamed of doing.

On the right-hand page is Olympic Gold Medalist Cheryl Miller. At right, Cheryl takes a jump shot while playing for the University of Southern California. Cheryl is now a coaching assistant at USC.

Photos courtesy Elise Kim

"America began as a dream, and without dreams, people can't reach their goals, because you have to look forward to something. You have to reach. You have to search for something. If you can see yourself doing it, if you can visualize yourself doing it, then you can achieve it. And in a dream, nothing goes wrong. And when you can put it in a reality and it goes right, then that's an accomplishment. But it all starts as a dream."

At right, Cheryl Miller and family are honored with a Cheryl Miller Night ceremony at USC. At the microphone is football star Lynn Swann. Below, a demonstration of Cheryl's winning spirit.

USC Sports Information

Courtesy Elise Kim

Study War No More

"We were just looking at the people today and remembering what they were like when they first began to come. Sometimes without any shoes on their feet, and just the clothes that they had when they left the camps. And it was November and they were shivering. . . . We had clothing distribution and they'd take anything that would fit no matter what it looked like, no matter what the color combinations. And they looked so ragtagged and yet so grateful."

The United States was created by immigrants, people who left the places where they were born to come to a new country. Immigrants have continued to pour in ever since. Barbara Reynolds is a woman who works with a very special kind of immigrant.

"And now we're getting waves of people coming from Asia—it's a very different situation from those who came from Europe. But the need is desperate and I'm very proud that our country is still receiving them, that there are people who are still trying to welcome them and to help them."

Probably the most terrible fact of the modern world is war. And one of the most terrible facts of war is that people are torn away from their homes. In a world that is divided up into countries, what happens to people who no longer have a country? Barbara Reynolds founded the Center of Hope to help, but she knows that the real answer is much larger.

"I dream of a world where people will care about one another and where they will be willing to share and to make sacrifices and not where some people think only of accumulating as much as they can while people next door to them are starving. And what I dream of is a time where nations will not lift up sword against nation and neither will they study war anymore. This is not a matter of treaties. It is not a matter of agreements to ban any kind of weapon. It's a matter of a change in the human heart."

Barbara Reynolds is shown with one of the young immigrants she has helped. This photograph was taken at a Center of Hope pot luck supper.

All the Gold in California

California is rich. It's rich in natural resources. It's rich in people. It's rich in ingenuity and opportunity and all the other things that make a state . . . well, rich.

To begin with, California is this country's leading farm state. And it has been since the middle of this century, when the state was only a hundred years old. But agriculture is not California's largest industry. Since 1919, manufacturing has made more money than farming. California is also one of the leading fishing states, is the center of the motion picture industry, is a major producer of petroleum, and just to round things off, still produces $16 million worth of gold every year.

Of course, as with most other states, the largest part of

The Hearst mansion in San Simeon.

Above, the fuselage of a DC-10 jetliner is assembled at Douglas Aircraft's Long Beach facilities.

California's gross state product comes from what are called services. Ever since the first storekeeper sold the first pick to the first prospector, retail sales have been a huge part of California's economy. And the state's location on the coast makes it a distribution center for the whole area.

Manufacturing produces the second largest part of California's income. Almost $95 billion worth of goods are produced here every year. That includes electronic components and communication equipment, aircraft, construction and farm equipment, and chemicals as well as many other products.

California's agriculture is amazing. The rich soil was only waiting for proper irrigation and, from around the turn of the century, it got it. Today, California produces more than $13 billion worth of crops and livestock every year. Except for tobacco, every major crop that is grown anywhere in the United States is grown commercially in California. By the 1950s, California was producing more than one-third of the nation's fruit and almost a third of the truck crops—vegetables raised for the market.

California leads in the production of more fruits, vegetables, and nuts than can be named here. But just beginning to list them makes your mouth water. There are almonds, apricots, lemons, grapes, plums, prunes, walnuts, olives, dates, figs—the list goes on.

About a third of California's farm income comes from livestock—beef and dairy cattle, poultry, sheep, and other animals.

California Bureau of Land Management

At right, cattle grazing at Spanish Flat. Below, grapes are dried in the sun to make raisins.

California Raisin Advisory Board

Mining is also a major part of California's economy. Gold no longer leads the field as the state's most valuable mineral. That honor now goes to oil, but there is a lot of competition. California has more valuable minerals in workable form than any other area of its size in the world.

If all that were not enough,

At left, Mickey Mouse greets visitors at Disneyland. Below is Elizabeth Lake in Yosemite. At the bottom of the page is one of San Francisco's cable cars.

Van Ness Ave.. California
51
& Market Streets

California has a few more arrows in its bow. The movie industry, for example, employs half again as many people as mining. And about 100 million tourists a year come to California to spend more than $28 billion.

All the gold in California does not come in little yellow nuggets.

At right, a fan poses with Charles Bronson's star on the Hollywood Walk of Stars. Below, the famous beaches of southern California.

31

New and Old

"I was born in China, mainland China. My parents, both of them, are doctors. Also, we have four sisters. Most of us are all either doctors or nurses because my mother wanted us to be that kind of job."

Dr. Amy Chan was a doctor before she came to the United States from China. And her new country provided a challenge. Dr. Chan practices a form of med-i-cine that has been recognized for centuries in China, but which is only beginning to be used here. It is very old but very new to us. Dr. Chan is an acupuncturist.

"When we moved to this country, I tried to fly everywhere to see which

Acupuncture needles are shown in front of an acupuncture chart. The chart shows the points at which needles should be inserted in the skin to affect particular areas of the patient's body.

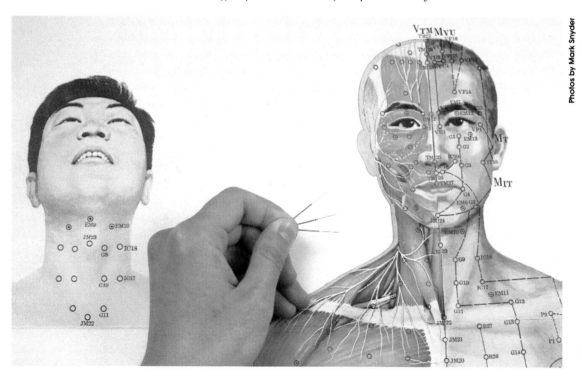

Photos by Mark Snyder

state they would accept acupuncturists. I tried go to Los Angeles. I tried to go to Chicago, because my husband was there. And then I found this area is good. People in this area, they realize acupuncture more and more. It's more popular. More and more they like the natural way to health."

Acupuncture is a way of treating illness that many people prefer to surgery or drugs. The doctor uses needles to pierce the skin of certain parts of the body. The body's reaction to the needles cures the disease or eases the pain. Acupuncture can be used with other forms of medicine as well. In fact, in China, surgery is often done without putting the patient to sleep with drugs by using acupuncture to numb the part of the body that is being operated on.

Dr. Amy Chan has found acceptance for her form of medicine in California. But she still thinks about the home she left behind.

"I enjoy my job very much, but I miss China so much. When I go to the Chinatown to buy the groceries or to have dinner or a meal there in a restaurant, then I enjoy all the Chinese food. It's a small town. You get everything from Chinatown."

There are many joys in the new, but nothing can ever completely replace the old.

Traditional Asian foods are for sale in a Chinatown grocery store.

33

Go West!

Americans have always gone west. In the beginning, west was the direction of new frontiers. After awhile, going west simply became a habit.

And some people would say that habit explains California. It's not that people in California come up with more strange, unusual, creative, and offbeat ideas than people in other parts of the country. It's that, wherever the ideas start, they always go west. When they get to California, they've gone as far as they can go unless they can tread water for a very long time. And so they stay.

In California, you can live pretty much the way you want to so long as you don't hurt anybody else. You can wear clothes you might get arrested for in other states. You can find classes

Tilesetter Simon Rodia created the Watts Towers.
Bits of broken glass are set in spires of concrete.

in almost everything, from the martial arts to new forms of meditation to the latest in basket weaving.

You—and ten thousand others —can come to California to be a movie star. You—and ten thousand others—can come to California to be a rock star. And it's not *quite* true that, in the words of the song, "All the gold in California is in a bank in the middle of Beverly Hills in somebody else's name." But on the other hand,

Novelist Jack London (left). San Diego de Alcala (below) is an example of mission architecture.

it's not exactly paving the streets, either.

And that's part of California culture.

There's another part that goes back to the Indians, to the missions, to the early Spanish settlers. This other part is made up of mission oak furniture, Indian pottery, and Spanish lace. Add into it silks and jade from China and Japan. Sprinkle it with gold dust and season it with Paris fashions ordered by San Francisco society to wear to the opera. It's the old California, the world Bret Harte wrote about and Jack London ran away from when it got too tame.

Bret Harte (at right) wrote realistically about life in California's mining camps and boom towns.

San Diego Convention & Visitors Bureau

Courtesy,
The Bancroft Library

Go down to the docks. This is where Asia comes to America and the dockworkers sweat in the golden California sun. Go to the factories, the canneries, the taverns. This is the world of John Steinbeck and William Saroyan.

Go out to the farms. This is the biggest farm state in the country, after all. There are more people out there, working to irrigate the desert and harvest the crops, than there are on the sound stage at Paramount.

All that's gold in California doesn't necessarily glitter.

Writer John Steinbeck (below) used California locales for many of his novels. Steinbeck's Cannery Row *is set among the fish canneries of Monterey (shown at right). Below, a view of springtime in wine country near Oakville. At far right is short story writer and playwright William Saroyan.*

MONTEREY
CANNING COMPANY

California Office of Tourism

Courtesy, The Bancroft Library

Imagine . . .

"I have to be many different people. I have to be a businessman sometimes and I'm pretty good at that, although it took some practice. And sometimes I'm a computer scientist and I talk to people in design and music and stuff about how computers fit into their worlds. And I'm all of those people, those are all real."

Jaron Lanier is part of a new breed. He's a computer whiz. He understands computers the way Rembrandt understood paint. And he's exploring the computer's possibilities with music.

"These instruments speak to the human body and to the human heart and computers will eventually. They have to. Right now the worlds generated by computers live mostly on television screens. I think in the future it will be really quite different. . . . Computers will be just generating a portion of our reality. . . ."

What will things be like if Jaron Lanier is right? It might begin with music, but where will it end up?

"There will be a certain portion of our environment that's physical and there will be another part that isn't. And it won't be obvious after awhile which is which. And what will be extraordinary then is that people will be generating their world by their imagination as well as the manipulation of physical matter, which is what they do now."

In other words, we won't just build houses, paint walls, and plant flowers. We will use computers to create imaginary gardens, to make walls that are white look red, to make music pour out of the nearest lamppost.

"And then what I think will happen is that people will communicate by immersing other people in their world. I mean, it'll just be this amazing thing, which we can't even begin to imagine yet."

If Jaron Lanier is right, computers will allow us to do the kinds of things we can only do now with books and paintings and other kinds of art.

"It'll be a very interesting world because instead of physical matter and wealth and machines being the things that create the world, it will be imagination. So imagination will be the most prized thing, much more important than gold."

It would be interesting to know whether Leonardo da Vinci thought the same thing.

Computer scientist Jaron Lanier.

Photo by Mark Snyder

Made for Myths

Myths are stories that are supposed to be true but actually aren't. Usually, they try to explain why things are the way they are. Sometimes, myths are about gods and imaginary creatures. Sometimes, they are things that ordinary people come to believe without really thinking about them.

California seems to be made for myths. Here's one: California is a good place to get rich. It's not hard to figure out how that myth got started. After all, there *was* all that gold. A lot of people *did* get rich in the gold rush. A lot more didn't, but the myth doesn't claim that everyone will get rich in California, just you.

Here's another myth: California is a good place to get famous. That one started with the movies and Hollywood.

A view of downtown Los Angeles.

The Hollywood sign above Los Angeles has become a symbol of the movieland that people dream about.

Of course, there are millions of people living in California and only a handful of them are famous, but remember the first thing about myths. They're stories that are supposed to be true and aren't. Usually, they have just a little bit of truth in them, enough to make them easy to believe.

So what other things do people say about California? Life is free. You can do whatever you want. They're all a bunch of kooks out there. The sun is always shining. Half the state is about to fall into the ocean. They're all vegetarians. They're all blondes. They're all healthy.

There are some states that don't have any myths. And then there are states like California that have

a lot more than their share. They're easier to find than nuggets in those old gold mines. What's hard to find is the truth. But maybe it goes something like this.

California is a place where there are people. People are people, no matter where you find them. The people in California are pretty much the same as people anywhere else. And California is not all that different from anywhere else.

Except, of course, that the sun always shines and the streets are paved with gold and everybody is blonde and they're all kooks out there and if you go to Hollywood you'll get to be a movie star and . . .

Important Historical Events in California

1540 The lower Colorado River is discovered by Hernando de Alarcón.

1542 Juan Rodriguez Cabrillo explores the coast of California.

1579 Sir Francis Drake lands in Trinidad or Bodega Bay to repair his ships and names the area Nuevo Albión.

1602 Sebastián Vizcaíno explores the coast and discovers the bay of Monterey.

1697 Jesuit missionaries enter Lower California and remain until 1767 when they are forced out by Charles III and their property is given to Franciscan monks.

1769 Spanish government occupies San Diego.

1772 Dominicans take over the missions and Franciscans go to Upper California.

1810 Revolution breaks out in Mexico and California remains loyal to Spain.

1812 Russians found Fort Ross.

1822 California becomes part of newly independent Mexico.

1823 Monroe Doctrine declares that there should be no more colonization in America by European powers.

1830 Hudson's Bay Company begins operations in northern California.

1831 Governor Victoria is thrown out of office.

1835 President Andrew Jackson offers to buy northern California. Offer is refused.

1836 Governor Mariano Chico is frightened out of the province and Governor Nicolás Gutiérrez is driven out of office.

1844 Governor Manuel Micheltoren is driven out of office.

1845 U.S. consul Thomas O. Larkin is told to encourage California to withdraw from Mexico. U.S. naval officers are told to occupy the ports in case of war with Mexico.

1846 The Bear Flag Revolt.

War breaks out between Mexico and the U.S. over Texas.

1848 Treaty of Guadalupe Hidalgo at the end of the Mexican War gives both Texas and California to the U.S. Gold is discovered at Sutter's Mill.

1850 California becomes the 31st state.

1864 During the Civil War, California remains in the Union.

1870 Rioting breaks out when Chinese workers fired by the Central Pacific flood the job market.

1906 San Francisco is hit by earthquake and fire.

1910 Hollywood is the movie capital of the world.

1930s Homeless people pour into the state looking for work during the Depression.

1941 After Pearl Harbor, Japanese Americans are herded into camps.

1965 Rioting breaks out in Watts section of Los Angeles during racial tensions.

1968 and 1972 Richard M. Nixon is elected president.

1971 Another major earthquake hits California.

1980 and 1984 Ronald Reagan is elected president.

California Almanac

Nickname. The Golden State.

Capital. Sacramento.

State Bird. California Valley Quail.

State Flower. Golden poppy.

State Motto. *Eureka* (I have found it).

State Song. I Love You, California.

State Abbreviations. Calif. (traditional); CA (postal).

Statehood. September 9, 1850.

Government. Congress: U.S. senators, 2; U.S. representatives, 45. **State Legislature:** senators, 40; representatives, 80. **Counties:** 58.

Area. 158,693 sq. mi. (411,013 sq. km.), 3rd in size among the states.

Greatest Distances. north/south, 770 mi. (1,239 km.); east/west 360 mi. (579 km.). **Coastline:** 840 mi. (1,352 km.).

Elevation. Highest: Mount Whitney, 14,494 ft. (4,418 m). **Lowest:** 282 ft. (86 m), in Death Valley.

Population. 1980 Census: 23,668,562 (18.5% increase over 1970), 1st among the states. **Density:** 149 persons per sq. mi. (58 persons per sq. km.). **Distribution:** 91% urban, 9% rural. **1970 Census:** 19,971,060.

Economy. Agriculture: beef cattle, hogs and pigs, poultry, milk, eggs, grapes, cotton, oranges, flowers, nursery products, hay, tomatoes, lettuce, strawberries. **Fishing Industry:** anchovies, salmon, tuna. **Manufacturing:** foods, transportation equipment, electric and electronic equipment, nonelectrical machinery, instruments, chemicals, petroleum and coal products, stone, clay, and glass products, clothing. **Mining:** cement, boron, petroleum, natural gas, crushed stone, sand and gravel.

Places to Visit

Death Valley Scotty's Castle at Death Valley.

Disneyland in Anaheim.

Marineland of the Pacific at Palos Verdes Estates.

Missions, throughout the state.

Redwood Highway, from San Francisco to Oregon.

San Diego Zoo.

San Simeon, near San Luis Obispo.

Annual Events

Tournament of Roses in Pasadena (New Year's Day).

Chinese New Year celebrations in San Francisco and Los Angeles (January or February).

Great Western Livestock and Dairy Show in Los Angeles (March).

State Fair in Sacramento (August and September).

Montery Jazz Festival (September).

San Francisco Film Festival (October).

California Counties

INDEX

MAR 1	DATE DUE		
MAR 15			
MAR 29			
MAR 31			
OCT 29			
JAN 20			
D-5			
MAY 15			
MAY 22			
MAY 30			
JUN 5			